# WORKING IN CLINICAL RESEARCH

## A Beginner's Guide for Research Nurses and Coordinators

ED CARBONELL

ISBN: 9798673231203

# CONTENTS

# Introduction

With the many fields and specialisations in nursing, clinical research is an exciting one. The scope of the job is wide ranging. It is challenging at times yet it can also be rewarding. The usual tasks are very different to the ones done in a ward set-up. There is an opportunity to explore other job functions like the ones in project management and laboratory science. The job has a multi-faceted role and you also become a part of something that is innovative.

When I first started to work as a research nurse, I had to learn new skill sets. A few of these were not taught in nursing school. I hope that with this book, I am able to share my experience to nurses and staff new in the field. This book can also be used by research coordinators who aren't nurses as both also share similar tasks (with a few exceptions). I wrote this book with the intention that it will equip novice research nurses and coordinators of the knowledge of what to really expect in the job. In this book I will talk about clinical trials (its phases and related terminologies), good clinical practice, the set-up of studies, and many more. Useful sample templates for clinical trials are also included in this book.

# Clinical research: a nursing opportunity

Nurses can play an important role in clinical research. It's a specialty that involves far more than the usual bedside duties and seeing patients on the wards. Responsibilities might include, for example, working with biological samples (ie separating blood plasma in the laboratory), project and data management, and writing research-related documents.

When we talk about research, we always think of paperwork. However, an experienced research nurse will tell you that, far from being a deskbound job, clinical research means being on the go all the time: in the laboratory working with centrifuges, dry ice and pipettes; out and about managing various projects; and even attending meetings abroad. The job can be as varied or as specialised as the project requires and offers the opportunity for nurses to develop a wide skill set.

# SO WHY CLINICAL RESEARCH?

Clinical research plays an important role in the advancement of medical knowledge. Through research, scientists can see how diseases affect the human body, how genetics influence certain disorders and how new drugs work.

All new technologies rely on the contributions made by research and in the field of medicine, the evolution of drugs and medical products is now more complex and faster moving than ever.

# THE RESEARCH NURSE: DIVERSE ROLES

Clinical research nursing is a broad field and so are the functions of the clinical research nurse. The clinical research nurse works by coordinating studies and the function of the role is very different from that of the nurse researcher. According to Jones (2015) of the *Nursing Times*, the involvement of the nurse in research has grown and the roles of the **clinical research nurse** and a **research nurse** vary considerably.

The clinical research nurse has a multifaceted role, which can include the coordination of studies from start-up to the archiving and maintenance of documents, study-related visits to research participants (also called **subjects** or patients), and the administration of clinical trial drugs. Clinical research nurses also ensure that all regulatory and governance documents are in place before the start-up of the study and take part in the closure of projects..

The nurse researcher, on the other hand, is primarily involved in the acquisition of new knowledge: proposing research questions, writing research methodologies, and developing the research project. Despite the differences, both roles can still overlap, since the clinical research nurse may also engage in the authorship of a particular study, aside from just coordinating.

# What is meant by coordinating ?

Study coordination involves a broad range of functions and tasks, such as undertaking feasibility studies (to ensure that the project is fit for purpose), attending various meetings and initial set-up of a project.

Coordination also involves organising lots of documents relating to study policies, regulations and standards. Other coordination tasks might include data collection, ordering laboratory kits, scheduling visits, working with different professionals such as doctors and nurses, and inviting study subjects to participate. The variety of tasks requires a broad organisational skill set that would include presentation and communications know-how and a good knowledge of office procedures. Further training would also be required for additional laboratory skills such as centrifugation or the storage and transport of biological samples.

# The Clinical Research Nurse: No two days the same

Listed below are typical criteria one might find in a clinical research nurse job description. Some of the terminologies might be unfamiliar, but these will be discussed in the later parts of this book.

- Upholding the principles of Good Clinical Practice (GCP)
- Assisting in the set-up of research studies
- Assisting in the closure of research studies
- Maintaining site file documents
- Attending site feasibility visits from study sponsors
- Obtaining and/or assisting investigators in obtaining informed consent from study participants
- Conducting study visits and study procedures related to a clinical trial. This may include procedures such as venepunctures, taking an ECG reading and performing other study-related procedures written in the study protocol.

- Administering trial medications and monitoring the health of study participants
- Managing study questionnaires
- Safety reporting involving the recognition of adverse events, severe adverse events, SUSARS and the proper documentation and reporting of such events
- Entering the collected study visit data on case report forms (paper and electronic)
- Assisting the clinical research associate (CRA) in site monitoring visits
- Resolving queries on case report forms
- Attending investigator meetings
- Assistance in developing the study costings for the site
- Performing laboratory techniques related to the study

The job description will give you an idea of the day-to-day life of a clinical research nurse, whether it's in the office or the clinical area. Given the broad range of responsibilities, it's safe to say that no two days will be the same. A typical day might include, for example, answering emails, conducting study visits with participants, including face-to-face interviews, obtaining the informed consent of participants, administering questionnaires and involvement with logistics planning and so forth. To make the best of the working day and to make sure that no time is wasted, it is important to list down the tasks and identify which will require immediate attention. Prioritising will help save time promote productivity.

# WHAT IS A CLINICAL TRIAL?

According to the World Health Organization (2018) a clinical trial is:

> *"Any research study that prospectively assigns human participants or groups of humans to one or more health-related interventions to evaluate the effects on health outcomes.*
>
> *Interventions include but are not restricted to drugs, cells and other biological products, surgical procedures, radiological procedures, devices, behavioural treatments, process-of-care changes, preventive care, etc."*

Clinical trials are types of research that study innovative treatments, drugs or medical devices. They look at the safety, side effects and the effectiveness of treatments with the goal of improving patient care. If a new drug is being developed, this will be studied first before it becomes licensed and before it goes into the market, which could take years. The drug company or developer (sometimes called the **sponsor**) will implement randomised clinical studies involving the recruitment of healthy volunteers and patients. The volunteers will then be asked to take the drug either in placebo form (meaning something that is not the drug), or the actual drug, depending on the design of the study. This is a common clinical trial design, called a **double-blind study**. A double-blind study simply means that neither the participant nor the clinical researcher knows whether the drug assigned is a placebo or not. There are many different study designs and a double-blind study is just one example. If the research participant and the researcher know that the drug taken by the volunteer is the actual drug itself, then it's called an **open-label study**.

## Phases of Clinical Trials

Clinical trials are divided into four phases, as follows:

- **Phase I:** These are small-scale studies, usually involving around 10-100 participants or subjects (Highleyman, 2005). The participants are at most healthy volunteers and the drug or medical product is monitored for side effects or toxicities. If it is a drug being tested, a small dose is usually given to the participants. If all goes well, the dose will then be escalated to a slightly higher level (Cancer Research UK, 2015).

- **Phase II:** This is still small-scale, but it may involve a larger group of up to several hundred participants. The participants invited into this phase of the study have the actual illness or disease. The study looks at establishing acceptable dose levels. It will also continue to monitor safety, efficacy and take note of possible side effects (U.S. Food & Drug Administration, 2018).

- **Phase III:** This phase will involve hundreds to thousands of participants with the actual disease being studied. The studies in this phase may compare new treatments to what is already available in standard care (Eldridge 2018). The study will still continue to monitor the drug's efficacy as well as its safety and side effects. Since on this occasion the drug is tested in an even larger population, rare side effects are more likely to be observed. Regulatory authorities (such as the Food and Drug Authority for the US) usually require phase III data before approving new medications for licensing. Roughly around 20 to 30 per cent of the trial medications in phase III move to phase IV (Weatherspoon, 2018).

- **Phase IV**: Over time, more data will be revealed about the drug being studied. The drug or medical product being trialled has now received its licence. Additional studies will also be implemented in this phase to monitor how it works in the long term as well as to collect information on the even rarer side effects. This is the phase where post-marketing studies take place (Highleyman, 2005).

# Good Clinical Practice

The development of clinical research studies is always geared towards providing good benefits for the public. In order to ensure that the research is ethical, it is imperative that the principles of Good Clinical Practice (GCP) are applied at all times, without exception. Applying GCP principles provide assurance that studies are consistently centred on patient safety as well as protecting patients' rights.

The UK government website GOV.UK (2014) defines Good Clinical Practice as "a set of internationally-recognised ethical and scientific quality requirements that must be followed when designing, conducting, recording and reporting clinical trials that involve people." Complete guidance on Good Clinical Practice can be found in the International Council for Harmonisation (ICH) website, which is periodically updated.

Applying the principles of GCP ensures that before we conduct or implement the clinical trials as clinical researchers, we must be educated and trained to conduct the study safely. We must ensure that an informed consent is obtained from the participant prior to performing any task in the study. Patient confidentiality must be observed at all times and we should act as the patient's advocate when it comes to protecting their rights and making sure that they are safe at all times.

The 13 Principles of ICH Good Clinical Practice are available on the ICH GCP website (https://ichgcp.net/2-the-principles-of-ich-gcp-2/). They are also mentioned in the Guidance for Good Clinical Practice document produced by the European Medicines Agency (https://www.ema.europa.eu/en/human-regulatory/research-development/compliance/good-clinical-practice.) For more detailed information, you can refer to those websites.

According to good clinical practice:

→ Clinical research studies must abide by the ethical principles consistent with good clinical practice

➜ Risks should be evaluated against the anticipated benefit before a clinical trial study is started. A study should only be initiated if the benefits outweigh the risks.

➜ The rights, safety, & well-being of the study participants must be the most important aspect of every clinical trial study

➜ Clinical trials should be written in a well-detailed and well-described manner

➜ All individuals involved in conducting clinical trials must have received proper training before performing its related tasks

➜ Clinical trials should be compliant with regulatory and ethics board requirements

➜ All participants of the study must have provided their informed consent before actually participating

For more detailed information on Good Clinical Practice, see the European Medicines Agency website: https://www.ema.europa.eu/en/human-regulatory/research-development/compliance/good-clinical-practice .

# GCP CERTIFICATION: A MUST

Before engaging in any clinical research study, the research nurse as well as all research staff must receive training on Good Clinical Practice. A **GCP certificate must be obtained**, without exception. Trainings can be done face-to-face through GCP classes or workshops and it can also be completed online. In some cases, the sponsor of a study, the institution or the company will conduct their own GCP training. The certificate must be renewed on a regular basis, usually every two years, but some sponsors or companies require renewal annually.

# Types of Research Studies

It is important to note that there are numerous types of research studies and that some of these overlap with each other. The following below are study types that the research nurse will most likely encounter in their practice:

1. **Portfolio studies** - These are studies that received funding via a rigorous application process conducted by a specific organisation or research network. The studies are registered as a part of the organisation's portfolio. The study could be either commercial or non-commercial. In the UK, the National Institute for Health Research (NIHR) has a portfolio of studies that consists of research that can be searched online. For a study to be considered as part of their portfolio, the study has to meet certain eligibility criteria before a decision on funding is made (NIHR, n.d.).

2. **Academic studies** - These are studies from universities such as studies conducted by a PhD student.

3. **Observational studies** – These studies are so-called because the intention is to merely observe: no manipulation or intervention is applied to initiate a desired effect. An example would be a study of the effects of smoking on the lung capacities of a certain population. No treatment is applied and the investigator aims only to identify the effects of smoking on lung capacity through the collection of data from the observations of a sample population..

4. **Commercial studies** - These are studies sponsored by private companies (eg pharmaceutical companies). Commercial studies may be interventional, as in clinical trials, or they may be observational, but they must be privately sponsored.

## Members of the Clinical Trials Research Team

The success of a clinical trial is the result of the efforts and contributions made by each member of the research team. Some studies might involve various members on a global scale. No matter how vast the geographical coverage of any given research study, the terms below are still widely used to identify team members and their particular functions.

- **Sponsor:** According to the Health Research Authority (2018), a sponsor is:

*"an individual, company, institution, organisation or group of organisations that takes on the responsibility for initiation, management and financing (or arranging the financing) of the research."*

Examples of such sponsors might include a pharmaceutical company that began a clinical trial study and wants to run the study at specific sites such as a hospital or clinic.

- **Chief Investigator (CI):** The Chief Investigator is usually a medical doctor assigned by a sponsor to oversee the overall status of a clinical trial study. They are designated as responsible for the design, conduct and reporting of the study.

- **Principal investigator (PI):** Usually a medical doctor designated to oversee the overall status of a clinical trial study at a specified site. In some cases, the Chief Investigator is also the Principal Investigator, especially in studies that run only at a single site. For multicentre studies (meaning a study conducted at various centres or clinical trial facilities), there will only be one Chief Investigator, who oversees all the studies being run at different sites. There will then be a Principal Investigator at each site (only one PI per site).

- **Sub-investigator/Co-investigator:** The sub-investigator helps the principal investigator in terms of the design and implementation of the study. When a principal investigator is not available due to other duties at some point, the sub-investigator may perform the functions of the principal investigator, such as obtaining informed consents, performing physical assessments and conducting other tasks as approved by the principal investigator. The responsibilities of a sub-investigator must be specified clearly on the delegation log.

- **Research Site Manager:** The research site manager manages the day-to-day operations of the studies at a specified site or clinical facility. This role may have various job titles such as research operations manager, study manager, etc. The research site manager might also "line-manage" other members of the team.

- **Research Nurse:** Coordinates the study and may perform study visits and clinical tasks specified in the study's protocol such as phlebotomy, electrocardiogram (ECG) monitoring, taking of vital signs and so forth. The role of the research nurse also depends on the job description specified by the employer, but specific to the research nurse's role is the ability to perform clinical skills and administer study medications such as intravenous medications, and patient monitoring in trials involving infusions drugs. Any other research coordinator would not be able to administer intravenous medication, as special training and a licence to practise is required for such procedures, e.g. a registered nursing licence.

- **Research Coordinator/Research Assistant:** This team member coordinates the study and may perform study visits, as long as the tasks are within their scope and are clearly documented in the delegation log. There are some tasks that can only be performed by a registered health care professional, such as administering infusions. Such specific tasks are only to be performed by research nurses or research physicians (sub-investigators or principal investigators, if they are medical doctors themselves).

- **Data Manager:** Manages the overall data of the study on site. This may include transferring the data written on paper (e.g. questionnaires, patient notes etc.) to spreadsheets or case report forms. Some sites do not have a data manager and thus the research coordinator or the research nurse may perform data management duties.

# Patient (Participant) Confidentiality

A large amount of data is collected during clinical research, which can include a lot of information about the participants. Depending on what is being asked in the study protocol, the research nurse will be collecting data such as age, date of birth, medical and surgical history of the participants, as well as a record of conversations that may contain sensitive information. It is very important that only the necessary data is collated and that it is used solely for the purpose intended. Furthermore, all data collected should be treated as confidential.

## How do we ensure patient confidentiality?

Firstly, before any data collection takes place, an informed consent is obtained from the participant. The responsibility for this task depends on the study protocol and the policies of the research site. Most of the time, it is the doctor or the principal investigator who obtains consent. The research nurse should not assume this responsibility if he/she is not delegated to obtain it, especially if the trial involves medicines. However, a nurse or coordinator can witness and assist the doctor by providing information to the participant as to what the study is all about and what to expect when they participate. This ensures that participants will have made an informed decision and also makes sure that they understand what they are participating in.

During the process of obtaining a participant's informed consent, confidentiality is explained. Efforts must be made so that the participant understands that all personal identifiable data collected during the study will be kept confidential and that information will only be shared with research individuals who are directly involved in the participant's care, such as the research doctor, the research nurse or the clinical trials practitioner and the research coordinator. The participant will also be assigned a study number to anonymise his or her name.

## Anonymising Participant (Patient) Identifiable Information

The practice of anonymising participant identifiable information is very important. Policies must be in place to maintain patient confidentiality. One direct example of anonymising patient-identifying information is by assigning a subject number to a patient. This number will be used to identify the patient when data is shared to sponsors, rather than using the patient's name. Patient information shouldn't be shared with study sponsors when reporting the relevant collected research data. The patient's identity must never be made known to study sponsors.

When collecting research data, we should only collect necessary important information. When it comes to reporting the data, whether it be in paper or electronic form (e.g. case report forms), a subject number or code is used instead of using the participant's name. The subject code can be in the form of numbers or letters. An example of this is XAL-10035. This example is a combination of letters and a hyphen followed by numbers. Depending on how a subject code is structured in the study, the first three letters could refer to a study code (XAL), the first digits could be the site number (10), and the last digits could be the subject number (035), which may mean that the participant is the 35th recruited participant for the study in the site. There's no specific rule for this formula and the structure depends on the study sponsor's preferences. The sponsors won't have any knowledge of the participant's name. They will only be provided a subject code or number associated with the research data collected for that participant.

As an example, if I were to be a study participant, instead of using my name Ed Carbonell, I could be assigned a subject number that may appear as 1111-111XX. This is the code that will be used when sharing my information with study sponsors. How the subject number appears depends on the sponsors and they can use letters or numbers.

# Setting up of Studies

There are several stages and documents involved in the setting up of studies. Having the correct paperwork in order is particularly important at this point, including all the government requirements, such as ethics approvals, and all the approval documents provided by your study site's research governance office. Any pending documents must be followed up and any missing documents requested by your research governance office must be submitted. The paperwork needed varies from country to country and from site to site. It is best practice to familiarise oneself with all requirements and to ensure that the compliance checklists are complete before giving the go-ahead for the start of a study. A summary of the relevant stages follows:

## Study Protocol

This is an essential document as it details the requires steps to perform the study. It's the study 'Bible' as it contains all the necessary information about how the study is going to be implemented and the eligibility criteria of the participants. It can serve as a manual for the study coordinators and research nurses as the protocol outlines what should be done on the study schedule visits (Health Research Authority, 2018).

## Feasibility

A feasibility review ensures that the study can be implemented successfully on site.. A feasibility review would include collecting information about the site's facilities, resources, and manpower. A feasibility review is usually carried out by the sponsor or their representatives on a site visit, but can also be conducted by telephone or by completing a feasibility form. The aim is to determine whether or not the study is likely to be successful, operationally and in terms of recruitment targets.

The sponsors will look at the chosen site and check if the facilities and resources required by the study are available and accessible. For example, if a participant has to undergo a colonoscopy procedure within a specific timeframe, the sponsors need to make sure that there is an endoscopy unit for colonoscopy and that it is accessible for the recruited participants. If you are involved in feasibility reviews as a research nurse or coordinator, it is best practice to prepare for any possible questions and to familiarise yourself with the facilities at your site.

## Site Selection

Once the sponsors are satisfied with the feasibility review, a site selection is made.

## Site Initiation Visit (SIV)

Site initiation visits or SIVs are implemented once the site has been selected. Sponsors or their hired representative (sometimes called a clinical research associate, or CRA) may conduct the site initiation visit, usually involving a meeting between the sponsors and the study team. SIVs may also involve training the research team about the study and this also includes training the principal and sub investigators. Signing of delegation logs will also be expected. A **delegation log** is a document that details what tasks each research member is allowed to perform .

## Regulatory Documentation and Approvals

### 1.   MHRA / FDA documents

If a clinical trial that takes place in the United Kingdom requires regulatory documentation from the Medicines and Healthcare Products Agency (MHRA). An example of such a document is the clinical trial authorisation or the CTA.

In the United States, the Food and Drug Administration (FDA) has authority over clinical trials. The FDA also evaluates medical products before they are marketed. It is important to ensure that FDA-related documentation is in place when setting up a clinical trial study.

If the clinical trial originates in the USA and is also implemented in the UK, the UK site must ensure that both MHRA and FDA documentation is in place. You should ask the study sponsors for copies of these documents so that you can file them in your site file. More information can be found on the MHRA and FDA websites. If you are setting up a study in another country, make sure that regulatory documents from agencies that have authority over clinical trials in that country are in place. You should be able to clarify which documents are needed through your site's research governance office.

## 2. HRA / IRB documents

One of the functions of the Health Research Authority (HRA) in the UK is to make sure that a research study is ethically reviewed and approved (HRA, 2017). In the United States, the Institutional Review Board (IRB) is an organisation that also approves and rejects clinical research bids. They ensure that the human rights and welfare are protected in the trial (U.S. Food and Drug Administration, 1998). Both HRA and IRB documents, applicable to the host country, should be in place when setting up a study.

## Research Governance

The University of Bath (2019) defines research governance as:

> *'The broad range of regulations, principles and standards of good practice that exist to achieve, and continuously improve, research quality across all aspects of healthcare in the UK and worldwide'*

A research facility usually has its own research governance office where documents on health-related studies can be reviewed. As a research coordinator/nurse, you would be expected to liaise frequently with research governance officers, as they maintain a set of compliance checks based on the site's research governance policies. It is also the research governance office that declares when any given study is open for recruitment. The start date for recruiting participants is also known as the **greenlight date**. It is important to take note of this, as sponsors will set recruitment targets. It is best practice to ensure that the site is able to recruit its first participant for the study within one month of the greenlight date.

## Site Targets

When setting up a study, a sponsor will ask how many participants your site can recruit from the greenlight date to the recruitment end-date. Coordinators may also be asked to fill a form specifying the target number. Meeting with your research governance office is essential here, so that you can discuss how your site is going to achieve the initial recruitment targets. Assessment of your research facility and the number of patients that your clinical site can cater for is key to identifying recruitment targets. If a site is not able to achieve the initial targets, this may be viewed negatively by sponsors and might result in them having second thoughts about opening future studies in your site. However, this may not always be the case, as there are also studies that can be really challenging, resulting in very difficult recruitment issues, as in studies where there is a very specific inclusion criterion. It is always best to discuss the targets with the team so that you can inform the sponsor of a realistic number of recruited participants.

## Greenlight Date/Site Study Activation

The greenlight date, also known as the recruitment start date, happens when all the necessary documentations related to the study are in place. This documentation includes the protocol, all the regulatory documents, documents related to protocol amendments (there may be several versions), the informed consent forms, participant information sheet, and all other paperwork that the research governance office may require. All these documents or their copies must be placed on the investigator **site file** – a folder that contains all the documents related to the study. It is possible to have several folders for the site file as there is often a lot of paperwork. Once these documents are in place and a site initiation visit has also been conducted by the sponsor, and with staff training already implemented, site study activation will take place. This means that the site is now ready for recruitment. Sponsors should be informed ahead as soon as the greenlight date is known.

# Clinical Trials

The following list includes terminology and other aspects of working on clinical trials that the research nurse might encounter.

## Blinded Studies

A lot of clinical trials involving medications are blinded studies. What this means is that both researcher and the recruited participant does not know whether the drug being dispensed is the trial drug or a placebo. This study is called a **double-blind placebo controlled study**.

## Primary and Secondary Endpoints

Endpoints are also known as the objectives or aims of the study. In clinical trials, endpoints are structured as either primary and secondary. The results of the study are primarily measured according to whether the trial drug was effective or not. This is the **primary endpoint** – the most important question in the trial. Clinical trials are developed to test whether the medical product works. If it is a comparative study, the aim is to see if drug A is more effective than drug B. Secondary endpoints are additional objectives of interest (Glen, 2017).

## Inclusion and Exclusion Criteria

Clinical trials will focus on a specific subject population, depending on the intentions of the research. Recruited participants are assessed according to the study's inclusion and exclusion criteria. The criteria have to be specified in order to identify the best candidates for the trial (e.g. patients with cardiac problems only for a cardiac trial drug). The inclusion criteria are those characteristics that your participant population should have, such as: currently experiencing the illness or disease being studied; age range; gender; specific laboratory values upon screening, and so forth. If the participant being invited for the study does not meet the inclusion criteria, then they must be excluded from the study. This is all done at the screening visit, which is usually the first study visit or appointment that the participant will make after signing the informed consent.

## Clinical Trial Investigational Medical Products

Clinical Trial Investigational Medical Products (CTIMPS) can either be a drug or a device such as a medical machine that will be used on participants. If the clinical trial involves giving a drug to the participant, then the research nurse must understand how drug dispensing works, as well as the concept of drug accountability. Drugs or medications come in different forms and routes, the most common being oral drugs, injections through intramuscular or subcutaneous routes, topical drugs applied to the skin, such creams and lotions, and the intravenous route.

There are particular types of drugs that only a licensed medical professional such as a doctor or a nurse is allowed to administer, an example being intravenous (IV) medications. In order to administer an IV drug, an IV cannula must be inserted into a patient's vein and the medication is given through this route. **Only trained medical professionals with a licence can carry out this procedure.**

## Drug dispensing

Clinical trial drugs are initially kept, stored and dispensed by the facility's pharmacy. The pharmacists storing clinical trial drugs must be trained in clinical research and clinical trials, since the approach will be different from that of dispensing standard drugs. Some studies require blinding and the pharmacist may dispense a placebo or the real drug itself, based on the randomisation that was generated when the participant entered the study. This will also require the pharmacist to use online computer programmes to dispense, such as **the Interactive Web Response System** or the **IWRS**.

It is the duty of the research nurse or coordinator to inform the pharmacists about the participant's study visit as well as to inform them that a drug needs to be dispensed on a particular visit. This will give the pharmacists ample time to prepare and it also allows double-checking of the availability of the drugs.

On the day of the study visit requiring drug dispensing, the research nurse or coordinator may also need to deal with IWRS systems online, using personal log-ins. This will electronically generate a prescription informing the pharmacist to dispense the study drug. When you involve yourself in a study dealing with IWRS systems, you will be trained in their use and log-ins will then be provided. **Make sure this is done before the study's greenlight date.** Also, dispensing should only be authorised when the assessments implemented in the study visit indicate that it is safe to do so. This involves completing the study tasks for that visit, which may usually involve a doctor assessing the participant and making sure that no adverse events have taken place when the participant took the trial drugs previously.

## Drug accountability

Drugs may be dispensed containing several tablets or drugs in one package. It is important to take note of the essential information and document the serial number, batch number, and expiry date of each packet. The research nurse should also count the remaining medications or tablets in the medication bottle or package during the visit to confirm that a dose was not missed. For example, if an oral drug is to be taken 'one tablet once a day' and the package given contains 30 tablets, we then expect 5 tablets remaining on the package if the next visit happens after 25 days. This is to ensure that the participant is taking the drug correctly and is not overdosing or under-dosing himself/herself.

## Case Report Forms

Study visits will involve data collection procedures, which consist of recording participant's vital signs, their answers to questionnaires, the physical assessment findings of the doctor and etc. Once the information has been collected, this will then be documented on the source notes (the patient's medical notes, in this instance) and on the **case report forms (CRF),** which can either be paper-based or electronic. The case report forms are then submitted to the sponsor. Participants' names are not written on CRFs – a subject number is used instead. Electronic case report forms (ECRFs) are more convenient because they speed up submission of recorded data. Data clarifications can then take place immediately, as soon as mistakes or discrepancies spotted by sponsors or their representatives have been corrected.

## Example of an ECRF:

| Subject ID | | Visit Schedule No. | |
|---|---|---|---|
| Date of Visit | | Time of visit: | |
| Physical Examination | ☐ Normal<br><br>☐ Abnormal. Please specify: | | |
| Lying Blood pressure | BP: | Oral temperature in Celsius | Temp: |
| Respiratory Rate | RR: | Pulse Rate | PR: |
| Drug Dispensed | ☐ Yes<br><br>☐ No | | |
| IWRS randomisation number | | | |

This is a basic example of a CRF, but most studies require more information and CRFs can consist of several pages if paper-based. If the sponsor requests a paper-based CRF it can be scanned, posted or faxed. It is important to always keep a copy of the CRF on site for reference purposes, in case data clarification is needed.

## Clinical Trial Vendors

The sponsor of a study may purchase computer software, electronic equipment or services from private companies that are sometimes referred to as vendors. Examples of packages obtained from vendors are electronic case report forms, ECG machines and laboratory kits. There will be times when there's an issue with the equipment or the service offered. It is best practice therefore to take note of vendor contact information.

## Laboratory Techniques and Dry Ice Handling

Sometimes, the research nurse/coordinator may be expected to perform several procedures outside of their skill set. Research nurses will also have to learn new skills such as using centrifuge machines, separating blood plasma from blood collection bottles, handling of dry ice and carrying out other laboratory techniques. Training should be provided. It is also the responsibility of the research coordinator or research nurse to study the protocol, so that unfamiliar tasks can be identified and training provided.

## Handling and Transporting Biological Samples

Researchers who package and handle biological samples such as blood or tissue specimens for shipment are required to show proof of training for this role so that they comply with the relevant law governing the study site. Biological samples not packaged and handled correctly pose a significant safety risk. Depending on the contents, the samples may be infectious, or contaminated when improperly handled. Study sponsors require a copy of the training certificate when expected to handle, package, and send biological samples via courier.

## Dry Ice Handling

Dry ice is sometimes used in transporting biological samples to keep them cold. This assists in preserving the sample before it reaches its destination. If dry ice handling is new to you, ensure that you receive proper training as there are safety issues associated with its handling. Dry ice is made up of carbon dioxide ($CO_2$). When dry ice melts, the $CO_2$ gases are released, which can cause suffocation in a room with no exhaust or proper ventilation. In addition, dry ice is also very cold and shouldn't be held with bare hands as it can cause frostbite. Special gloves should be worn and these should be made available in your department if dry ice handling is involved. Playing with dry ice should be avoided, no matter how exciting the cloudy gases might seem!

## GP letters

General Practitioner (GP) letters are highly useful tools in communicating with the doctors of the participants. I use GP letters to inform doctors that the patient under their care is participating in a clinical trial study. It is important that GPs are made aware of the patient's status in the trial and it also helps them when their patients come for a check-up. When participants decide to take part in a trial, they should also be made aware that the trial team will inform their GP about their involvement.

GP letters can also be used to inform the patient's doctor about possible changes in patient's condition as a result of the trial. Additionally, it allows them to also know if the patient has experienced an adverse event. The sponsor usually provides a template of the GP letter and this should be approved by the research facility's research governance office. The template will also need a company logo at the top of the page and other requirements may also be included in the template such as the address and contact number of your office. Further information may also be required, depending on the site's research governance office.

## Study cards

Study cards are carried by participants to show their family doctor or any other doctor that they are participating in a clinical trial. The card provides information about the trial. The card can also be used to list upcoming study visits and other useful information. Below is an example of a study card:

**CARBONELL TRIAL**

Study number: edmc-111

SAMPLE ONLY

Carry this card at all times

FRONT

This patient is participating in a clinical trial involving the use of Carbonell-111 for the treatment of...<More information>

| | |
|---|---|
| Patient Study ID | |
| Study doctor | |
| Address | |
| For more info, pls contact | |

Screening Visit:
Visit 1:

Visit 2:
Visit 3:
End of trial visit:

SAMPLE ONLY

BACK

## Physical Assessment / Examination

Certain study visits in a trial require physical assessments: these are usually carried out by the study doctor. This procedure involves an examination of the different systems of the body to check if the physical changes or symptoms that the patient is experiencing are related to the study. As a research coordinator or nurse, you must ensure that you have informed the study doctor about the upcoming visit, and let them know whether a physical assessment is required. This will give the study doctor time to prepare.

## Source Documents

Source documents are the primary documents relating to the assessments and interventions that were implemented during a study visit. A source document is different from the case report form: the data that you write on a case report form will usually come from a source document, ie the patient's medical notes, vital signs monitoring sheet, nurse's notes, the original copy of the informed consent and other documentation files considered as primary. Source documents are very important because they are the basis of your case report forms. The documentation of study visits must be thorough and complete and should follow the principles of good record keeping.

# The Informed Consent

Considered to be one of the most important documents in clinical trials, this legal document is given to the participant and explained before they take part in a study. It should contain information about the trial, the study schedule, and inform the participant that participating in a clinical trial is voluntary. It should also be emphasised that they can withdraw from the trial at any time. For best practice, participants should be given reasonable time to read an informed consent so that they can discuss this with their families or partners should they wish to. The informed consent form can be amended from time to time after its approval, so it is important to ensure that the participant signs the most recent and approved version of the informed consent document. The participant's signature must be obtained by the principal investigator or sub-investigator, provided that this task is reflected in the delegation log. It is important for the study doctor to explain the study and the contents of the informed consent. The participant may ask a few questions and it is the doctors who are best placed to answer, especially if they are medically related queries. It is vital that the participant thoroughly understands the clinical trial and their rights. It must be highlighted to them that involvement is voluntary and that they can withdraw at any time.

It is common for an informed consent form to be several pages long. It may contain comprehensive information that explains the study and can also include an itinerary of study visits and procedures that will be involved. The last page of an informed consent is where you can find the **consent form.** The participant places his signature and initials to agreed statements on this page. The most common mistake is when subjects tick the boxes of the 'initials box' instead of really writing their initials. A tick is not acceptable, as it will be difficult to confirm whether the ticking was really done by the participant or by someone else.

## Example:

I understand that my participation is voluntary and will not affect my medical treatment and my legal rights in any way

I understand that I can withdraw from the study anytime should I change my mind

As a research nurse or coordinator, it is important for the consent form to be initialled, signed and dated by the participants once they have agreed to take part. The study doctor obtaining the consent from the participant should also sign and this should also be dated. Copies of the completed informed consent forms will then be made. A copy is then filed with the medical notes (which is the source document), another copy is for the participant, and another copy is sent to their general practitioner (GP,) and should also be accompanied by a GP letter. Make sure that the participant is aware that their GP will be informed of their trial participation. The original documents of the signed informed consent will be filed on the site file.

# The Study Schedule

The study schedule is a schedule of the study visits that participants will undergo in a clinical trial. This document is kept in the study protocol. The schedule will contain the tasks and procedures to be performed during the screening visit, randomisation visit, and other study visits. It should also contain the tasks and procedures implemented during the withdrawal and termination of visits. An example is provided on the next page.

| | Screening Visit (V1) | Randomi-sation Visit (V2) | Day 1 (V3) | Day 2 (V4) | Early Termination | Termination Visit |
|---|---|---|---|---|---|---|
| Informed Consent | X | | | | | |
| Vital Signs | X | X | X | X | X | X |
| Weight | X | | | | X | X |
| ECG | X | | | | X | X |
| Physical Assessment | X | | X | X | X | X |
| Eligibility Review | X | | | | | |
| Full Blood Count | X | | X | X | X | X |
| Blood chemistry | X | | | | X | X |
| Administer Study Drug | | X | X | X | | |
| Get randomisation number on IWRS | | X | | | | |

This is just an example as normally, a study schedule may have more than just two visits and more procedures will also be involved. The Early Termination visit happens when the patient withdraws from the study before all visits have been completed.

## Screening Visit

This visit happens to check the participant's eligibility to take part in the clinical trial, based on the study's inclusion and exclusion criteria. An informed consent must be obtained first before a screening visit takes place. Sometimes, the informed consent is obtained during the screening visit, which means that previous to the screening visit day, the participant was already given enough time to read the informed consent and decide. As mentioned earlier in this book, it is essential that participants are given enough time to read and discuss with others. This can take up to 24 hours or more. The key idea here is that participants should not be pressured into taking part. Researchers should always promote informed decisions.

In the screening visit, participants might undergo several tests, depending on what is required in the study (blood tests, urinalysis and etc). As a general rule, the informed consent must be signed and dated before proceeding with the other interventions in the screening visit. This visit should also offer participants the opportunity to ask questions and have the study explained again thoroughly.

The screening visit of the first participant recruited in a particular study can be quite challenging. Each new study implemented always has its new ways of doing things and early planning and preparation are essential if a visit is to run smoothly. Always plan the logistics ahead, as some screening visits involve coordinating with several departments, such as those studies that have invasive procedures (eg colonoscopies). Also ensure that all the laboratory kits are available, since in most trials only laboratory kits from chosen vendors are allowed. Obtaining kits may require making orders that take days to arrive. Issues in the logistics and flow of the visit can be sorted by planning ahead and identifying any possible challenges.

## Randomisation Visit

Once the participant has been screened and found to be eligible to participate in the trial, a randomisation visit will take place. In some studies, a randomisation visit is integrated into the screening visit. This usually happens for non-complex studies, as it only requires a few inclusion criteria. Most likely, the randomisation visit is a separate visit, since the results of some of the tests might take days to arrive.

During the randomisation visit, the patient will be randomised to a certain treatment group. For example, if the study was a double-blind placebo controlled trial, in which there are two groups with one group receiving the drug and the other group with the placebo, the participant would be randomised by computer and assigned to either a drug or placebo group. If the study is a blinded study, the researchers will only receive a randomisation number and neither the participant nor the researchers know whether the participant's status is in the treatment group or in the placebo group. The system used to randomise may either be computer-generated, eg on the IWRS system via a chosen software, or by other methods approved by the sponsor, which can involve the faxing of forms. This should be mentioned in the study protocol.

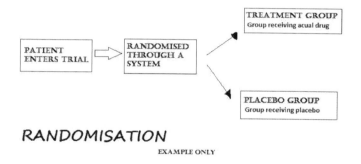

## RANDOMISATION

EXAMPLE ONLY

## Study Visits and Study Procedures

Clinical trial participants may be required to visit the clinic to undergo several procedures such as physical examination, blood test, answering questionnaires and receiving the study drug. These are called study visits. Sometimes, the visits can occur several times in a year (or even more), depending on what is written in the study protocol. I once worked on a study that required the participants to be in clinic at different scheduled times for a 52-week period. After that 52-week period, another year of study visits then took place, as it was required in the clinical trial.

From my experience, the key thing to remember when working with clinical trials in relation to study visits is to be prepared all the time. The research nurse or coordinator must ensure that all items, such as laboratory kits, are available in every study visit. These kits need to be ordered ahead from sponsors and deliveries can take time. It will be to the nurse's or coordinator's advantage if the availability of the laboratory kits is monitored, including the expiry dates. The team must also think of the logistics and manpower required for the visits, especially during the first participant visit, so that a framework on how future appointments will be implemented can be established. In addition, this will also assist in the smooth flow of the procedures and tasks to be conducted.

## Pharmacokinetic (PK) Sampling

Some clinical trials require the collection of blood samples at different points on a single patient study visit. PK sampling is done to check the drug levels in the blood after the study drug has been administered. Pharmacokinetics, by definition, is the process by which a drug moves within the body to achieve drug action after medication administration. There are four processes involved in pharmacokinetics: absorption, distribution, metabolism and excretion/elimination (Kee & Hayes, 2003). The research nurse or coordinator's involvement in PK sampling is the timed collection of a blood sample, applying phlebotomy skills. Research staff should not engage in venepuncture and phlebotomy without proper training. The training of this clinical skill should take place prior to the opening of studies that require blood collection. Institutions will have their own specific policies on this, in which most will require supervision and competency sign-offs for the first few venepuncture procedures performed. An example of a PK sampling form is shown on the next page.

| | |
|---|---|
| Collect blood before administration: | Time: _____ |
| Drug Administered | Time: _____ |
| Collect blood sample after 5 minutes | Time collected: _____ |
| Collect blood after 10 minutes | Time collected: _____ |
| Collect blood after 15 minutes | Time collected: _____ |
| Collect blood after 30 minutes | Time collected: _____ |
| Collect blood after 1 hour | Time collected: _____ |

This is just an example and the timings above may differ in the actual form as this depends on the study protocol.

Blood collections are required at different times and that means that the phlebotomy procedure will be implemented more than once. It is important to record the time accurately, as well as be on time in collecting the blood, to ensure the accuracy of the data from the labs.

## Withdrawal and Termination Visits

Sometimes, a subject may be withdrawn from the study. This means that they will be removed from the clinical trial study and they won't be able to continue with future visits and drug administrations. Reasons could simply be that the subject has chosen to voluntarily withdraw, or has become unwell following the trial (as in the case of an adverse event). The study doctor will decide for safety reasons if the subject is to be withdrawn from the trial due to a serious adverse event.

A termination visit is the last study visit of the subject, where all the required visits in the protocol have been completed. The next stage for the subject after the termination visit will be decided by the doctor (ie whether to give more clinical trial options or to refer the subject back to standard care). Subjects should not be left without a plan after the termination phase, especially if they were in the trial as a result of their ongoing illness. We must always think of their best interest as well as of their safety at all times.

# Site Monitoring Visits

In order to ensure that the data collected by the researchers onsite is accurate and recorded according to guidelines and protocols, a site monitoring visit will be necessary. These visits are conducted so that cross-checking of data can be made against the source documents and is usually implemented by a clinical research associate (CRA). A CRA acts as a liaison between the clinical trial sponsor and sites where the clinical trial is being run. The CRA is neither employed by the sponsor or the clinical site, usually from another company or agency to avoid any influence or bias and to maintain the integrity of the research work (MHA Online, 2019).

Site monitoring visits should be booked ahead by the CRA to the clinical site. It is important for the clinical site to prepare the items that the CRA needs for the visit. The items include source documents such as patient notes, case report forms (if they are on paper) and any source of documentation used in the data collection, such as laboratory and diagnostic reports. A workspace should be allocated for CRA use. The assigned research nurse or coordinator must also be prepared to answer their questions and clarify or correct any data that's inconsistent or incorrect. Data clarification or query resolutions are quite common during these visits and the principles of proper documentation must be followed when correcting mistakes in documented information, for instance by writing a line across the written words as well as placing the initials, signature, and date with the new information written just above. This also applies for written documentation. Digital documents can be corrected more easily, and the change of information will automatically be recorded by the programme or software used.

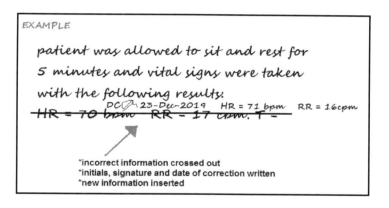

In some cases, a CRA may have already contacted the site and queried case report forms before the monitoring visit. The clinical site coordinators or research nurses must resolve these queries before the monitoring visit happens. For best practice, it is important to resolve the queries as soon as they are brought to attention, or within 3 to 5 working days, unless there is real urgency.

During site monitoring visits, it is possible that new queries will be opened up. While the CRA is on site, efforts must be made to resolve these new queries, as the CRA can provide guidance as to how to answer the queries properly.

**Things to prepare on a Site Monitoring Visit:**

+ Booking date of the site-monitoring visit (The CRA usually informs the site of their preferred date. PI availability should also be considered)

+ Source Documents such as patient notes, Case Report Forms and other related documentations (digital or paper)

+ Working space for CRA to use

+ Queries to be resolved before visit date

The CRA may also ask to speak to the research site's principal investigator (PI). The research nurse or coordinator must ensure that the PI is available on the monitoring visit date. Before the visit date is officially booked, communication with the PI should have been made so that the availability of both PI and CRA is considered and a convenient date for the visit can be noted.

# Investigator's Meetings

Sponsors of clinical trials may organise meetings about a particular study, usually inviting principal and sub-investigators from clinical sites. The coordinators and research nurses may also be asked to attend as representatives in the absence of their investigators. These meetings are conducted in chosen key locations such as major cities, thus requiring the representatives to travel. The purpose of the investigator's meeting is to introduce the study to investigators in great detail. Inputs coming from representatives and investigators may be obtained based on the agenda of the meeting, as well as on what is being discussed. The meetings may last a day or two, but this depends on how the pharmaceutical sponsors set it up. These events are also a great way for the investigators and researchers to network, thus establishing rapport with people involved in the making and running of the study.

Such events give research staff an opportunity to talk to the project and programme managers of the study, meet with key persons from the sponsor, have a chat with the chief investigator and the CRAs, as well as the research nurses and coordinators of other research sites. This is called networking. This is really helpful when issues arise during study implementation on your site. Having known people from networking makes it easier for you to contact them for help in finding solutions to study problems. It's possible that the problems encountered on your site are problems that have already been dealt with by others. Knowing more people in the field and taking time to consult them makes troubleshooting issues a lot easier. In addition, networking also helps build good working relationships with sponsors and other key persons in the study.

# Safety Reporting & Pharmacovigilance

In a clinical trial, subjects may experience adverse events. Some are mild and some are serious. The events may also be severe and life-threatening. This is why proper assessment, reporting, and management of the events is important. Safety should always be a priority. Before the drugs or medical products are tested on humans, safety will have already been established from pre-clinical studies, however the possibility or chance of the participants experiencing unique side effects and adverse effects are also possible.

## Pharmacovigilance Terminologies

A few special terms will be encountered in safety reporting. It's also possible that these terminologies might be redefined operationally, according to sponsor's preference. Should questions arise in your practice, such as being unsure whether to label a clinical trial event as a severe adverse event (SAE) or an adverse event (AE), it is best to clarify this with the study's clinical research associate (CRA), or the sponsor, in the absence of a CRA.

**Adverse event (AE).** Any untoward reaction event that may or may not be related to the clinical trial study.

A good example of an AE is when a study participant reports that they are experiencing a common cold. If the common cold happened while being active in the study, it will be recorded as an adverse event. Accurate reporting and documentation is necessary for any AEs and information such as the start date of the event, the time it happened, the end date and its level of severity should be noted (e.g. mild, moderate, or severe). A clinician may be needed to identify the severity of the AE.

**Severe Adverse Event (SAE)**. This is similar to AE, but has to be an event that is <u>life-threatening,</u> or which involves <u>hospitalisation</u>. This may or may not be related to the clinical trial study. Examples include developing severe life-threatening illnesses or experiencing major accidents while on the study, such as vehicular accidents. If the participant is hospitalised for whatever reason, this will also be considered as an SAE, unless the study specifies that such an event is not considered as SAE. Identifying SAEs needs clinician input. The research doctor (principal investigator preferably) must be involved in confirming the event as an SAE. Also, **as a general rule**, SAEs must be reported immediately to your principal investigator, study sponsor, and research governance office <u>within 24 hours</u> of the event being disclosed or at the time it was reported by the participant. This is an essential requirement and failure to comply could lead to serious penalties. Safety measures must also be in place at all times. A thorough assessment of the situation is of vital importance.

**Adverse Drug Reaction.** Any reaction that is related to the drug in the study.

**Near-miss.** Any event that almost caused harm or injury.

Preparing the wrong drug and **almost** giving it to the participant after being informed by a colleague that you prepared a different drug is an example of a near-miss event. Near-misses must be documented as well as reported through incident reports, so that such an event can be studied and systems put into place to prevent similar situations from happening again.

**Suspected unexpected serious adverse reaction (SUSAR).** As the term itself states, these are reactions that are suspected yet unexpected and serious.

Since it is suspected, the sponsors will usually have identified what the events might be: there should be a list available so that when such an event happens, they can be immediately identified as an SUSAR. Since SUSARs are also considered as serious events, the research coordinator or nurse, as well as the principal investigator, **must report the event within 24 hours.**

# Subject recruitment Strategies and Participant Adherence

Recruiting subjects for a clinical trial can be challenging. There are different opinions on how best to recruit study subjects. There are also different views as to how we can make them stay for the duration of the study. One of the best approaches is for the team to brainstorm on recruitment ideas together with the investigators. Some clinical sites hire a head of recruitment personnel, who then takes the responsibility on things that are related to subject recruitment. Sometimes this may also involve social media sites and advertising strategies to reach potential participants, provided that such a strategy has been approved by the ethics committee (e.g. HRA or IRB).

We'll now move on to implementing research meetings, attendance to multi-disciplinary meetings and using outpatient clinics as strategies for recruitment.

## Research Meetings

Meetings are a good opportunity for members of the research team to get together to discuss issues and find solutions to problems. Research meetings must involve all members of the research team, including the principal investigator. I used to work as a research nurse on a clinical site. We used to conduct research meetings at least once a week, each lasting only an hour or less. We invited the nurse specialists as well as other doctors who would like to participate in the studies. The more you network with people on your site, the easier it is to recruit study subjects, since nurse specialists as well as doctors can actually help you with your pressing recruitment problems. They can invite the patients that they see on standard care, depending on what is agreed with the research staff.

## Multidisciplinary meetings

If your clinical site is a big organisation such as a hospital, you will find it useful to attend multidisciplinary meetings. These meetings involve different members of the healthcare team (e.g. radiologists, other consultants, dieticians, physiotherapists, occupational therapists and nurses). The members will collaborate on patient cases. Multidisciplinary meetings are also a good venue to discuss active clinical trials with medical consultants, making them aware of the possible studies that their patients can participate in. The meetings also make it possible for the research nurse or coordinator to network with the consultants, as establishing rapport with key persons (such as nurse specialists and doctors) will really make your work much easier, especially in recruiting patients as possible study participants.

# Logistics Planning

Running a clinical trial involves meticulous planning, from ordering laboratory kits to creating positive experiences for participants during their visits. Several factors must be considered for effective planning such as: the facilities and equipment available, manpower (which includes research coordinators, nurses and doctors), and the ordering and auditing of laboratory kits.

## Facilities & equipment availability

Facilities and infrastructure refer to the availability of research clinics and clinical equipment, which is usually mapped out by the research staff at the time of feasibility. However, in some sites such as hospitals, research staff may "borrow" clinics from standard care for research use, which means that the clinics themselves are intended primarily for patients in the hospital and the researcher will only use the clinical rooms when they are vacant. Further planning needs to be involved here, such as communicating with the clinic manager way beforehand to obtain some heads-up. If the clinic spaces can be booked formally, then that will be much better. Rechecking the booking a day before, as well as on the day of the participant clinic visit, can be very helpful. As a research coordinator or nurse, you want a smooth flow of the participant's visit. Planning is definitely key in achieving this. If you need to ask permission from a department to use their facility and space, make sure that you organise this in advance.

Equipment for use in a clinical trial can range from the equipment used in monitoring participant's vital signs such as sphygmomanometers to monitoring heart rhythms such as the electrocardiogram machine. Other common machines also include the ones used in the laboratory, such as the centrifuge for processing biologic samples. If a particular piece of equipment is not available on your site, sponsors can sometimes provide this. Once again, such issues should be mapped out and identified at the time of feasibility. If the research staff need to borrow a particular machine to be used by study participants, make sure that permission is sought ahead of time.

Clinical trials also require machines to be calibrated and checked regularly at specified time points. The research nurse or coordinator should make sure that information related to calibrations is documented, as this will be needed in the CRA monitoring visits.

## Research staff manpower

All staff involved in a clinical trial must be trained and their names and responsibilities reflected in the study delegation log.

The research nurse or coordinator must think of contingency plans when the assigned staff is not available on a study visit as there's always a possibility that the staff member may be on emergency leave or unwell. One solution for issues like this is to train other staff in the clinical trial to serve as back-up in case of a manpower shortage emergency. Their names and responsibilities should also be reflected in the delegation log.

Another challenge that sites may face is the availability of the research doctor. The doctors may be stuck with seeing other patients at the time of study visit. While it is possible to let the participant wait for the doctor to come, this may not be a good experience for them. Efforts must be made to include the doctor in the communications of participant visits so that they can note this on their diary. Additional information should also be provided to the doctor ahead of time, such as specific physician tasks that will need to be performed, such as physical assessment, writing prescriptions, and other study-specific interventions.

Reminders must also be put in place, such as an email sent a week before and then a day before the study visit. While reminders may not necessarily be required as each individual should be responsible to record the schedules in their diaries,

74

some will still forget. In my experience, sending a reminder email a week and then a day before really helped.

## Ordering and auditing of laboratory kits

Laboratory kits will be specific to a particular study. Even if such equipment, such as blood collection bottles, is already available on site, some studies still require that you only use the equipment provided by the sponsor, as these will have been pre-packaged according to study visit schedules, with specific bar codes in place. Sending samples in containers not specified by the sponsors will risk the sample being destroyed by their central laboratories and the site will have to conduct another study visit and collect the biological sample again.

The site will have to order the sponsor-preferred laboratory kits ahead. The arrival of the kits can sometimes take days or weeks, thus it is best to plan the orders ahead. The laboratory kit must be available at the time of the study visit or else you'll have to explain to the study subjects that they will have to come back again for another visit because a laboratory kit was not available, which can be a hassle. Frequent audits of the kits should also be made so that the expiry date can be checked, enabling the site to order additional kits in advance.

The following questions will provide guidance in
evaluating the site's readiness to implement a clinical trial
study in relation to facilities, equipment availability and
manpower:

+ Does your clinical site have all the facilities needed to
  run the clinical trial effectively? Is there an available
  space or clinic room that can be designated solely for
  research use? If not, what are the alternatives? Do you
  need to inform the department ahead in order to
  borrow the required space?

+ Does your site have the equipment (e.g.
  sphygmomanometer, ecg machine etc.) needed solely
  for research use? If not, is there an alternative or can
  the research staff borrow them? Do you need to book
  the equipment or formally ask permissions from
  departments in borrowing the equipment?

+ Is there an allocated staff member available as back-up
  should there be manpower problems? Are the names of
  the staff for back-up documented in the delegation log?
  Are their responsibilities also documented in the
  delegation log?

🌢 Do you need to inform the research doctor ahead of an upcoming participant study visit? What systems are in place to remind the research doctors of the visit?

🌢 Do you have the laboratory kits available for all the clinical trial visits? How close is the expiry date? Do you need to reorder kits ahead?

# Close-Out Visits

When all study participants complete all their visits in a clinical trial and further participant recruitment is no longer required, a close-out visit will be conducted. This is coordinated by the site and the sponsor of the study. There are many reasons for the closure of a study on a site. For example:

1. All the study participants have completed their termination visits, which means that no succeeding visits will take place and no further recruitment will happen.

2. The site has not performed well in the recruitment phase to the point that no participants have been recruited in a given time period

3. The clinical trial drug or product has been withdrawn by the sponsor or regulatory agency due to untoward incidents that took place.

Close-out visits are really about formalising all the documents needed as well as ensuring that all the paperwork involved, such as documents and case report forms of the visits, are in order with all mistakes corrected. The visit is typically conducted by the CRA. The visit confirms that all identified queries have been resolved. The research nurse or coordinator should communicate with the CRA regarding any additional documents required, so that these can be provided immediately. The site files should also be complete, with the necessary documents in proper order.

# Useful Sample Templates for Clinical Trials

Generally, a clinical trial study will have its own template provided by the sponsor. The following templates below contain the basic information needed and can be used to develop your own template, should you need to make one. It is also possible to modify the layout of these depending on staff preference. In the absence of a sponsor-provided template, it is a good idea to make one to organise documentation as well as to help with query resolutions during monitoring visits.

## CONCOMITANT MEDICATION LOG

| MEDICATIONS TAKEN | DOSE & ROUTE | INDICATIONS | START DATE | STOP DATE |
|---|---|---|---|---|
|  |  |  |  |  |
|  |  |  |  |  |
|  |  |  |  |  |
|  |  |  |  |  |
|  |  |  |  |  |
|  |  |  |  |  |

# ADVERSE EVENTS LOG

| | | |
|---|---|---|
| Reported Event or Symptom | | |
| Severity | | |
| Start Date & Time | End Date & Time | |
| IMP related? | | |
| ACTION REQUIRED | | |

# TELEPHONE SUMMARY

I find telephone summaries or notes to be very useful in recording phone conversations. You can never rely too much on your memory. Taking notes in an organised way will help you with your work. Every time you make or receive a phone call (eg subject, doctor, CRA, sponsor or colleague) related to a clinical trial study, always take notes and file them accordingly as they can also serve as source documents should queries come up in the future.

## TELEPHONE NOTES

| Name of Caller | | Tel. # | |
|---|---|---|---|
| Received by | | Tel.# | |
| Date &<br>Time<br><br>of call | | | |
| Topic | | | |
| Message:<br><br><br>Name & Signature:     . | | | |

# PAST MEDICAL & SURGICAL HISTORY

Past medical and surgical history information is useful, especially when evaluating the subject's eligibility for the clinical trial. This can be handy when the trials have extensive inclusion and exclusion criteria. Furthermore, this is also helpful if the medical notes are still paper-based and the information that you need, such as illness history, is written on different pages on the medical record.

| MEDICAL HISTORY | | | | |
|---|---|---|---|---|
| Name of Illness / Diagnosis | Severity (Mild, Moderate, Severe) | Medications taken/ treatment procedures involved related to illness | Start Date | Stop Date / Date Resolved |
| | | | | |
| | | | | |
| | | | | |
| | | | | |

| SURGICAL HISTORY | | | |
|---|---|---|---|
| Name of Surgical Procedure | Indications | Medications taken (if any) | Date of Surgery |
| | | | |
| | | | |
| | | | |
| | | | |
| | | | |

# A Few More Words...

Clinical research is an exciting area for nurses to work in. It's a great way to build additional skills that are not taught in nursing school. The information in this book is based on experience as well knowledge gained from training and research. This book is just a starting point, as more knowledge will be gained from experience as you immerse yourself in clinical research jobs. When I began working as a research nurse, I had to start from scratch and had to learn the ins and outs of the job. There was no book to guide me. I hope this book will help those who are starting out on their first clinical research job.

# References:

Cancer Research UK. (2015). Phases of clinical trials. [online] Available at: https://www.cancerresearchuk.org/about-cancer/find-a-clinical-trial/what-clinical-trials-are/phases-of-clinical-trials.

Eldridge, L. (2018). What are the Phases of Clinical Trials?. [online] Verywell Health. Available at: https://www.verywellhealth.com/what-are-the-different-phases-of-clinical-trials-2249410.

European Medicines Agency (2020). Good clinical practice. [online] European Medicines Agency. Available at: https://www.ema.europa.eu/en/human-regulatory/research-development/compliance/good-clinical-practice.

Good Clinical Practice Network. (n.d.). THE PRINCIPLES OF ICH GCP. [online] Available at: https://ichgcp.net/2-the-principles-of-ich-gcp-2/ .

Health Research Authority. (2017). *What we do*. [online] Available at: https://www.hra.nhs.uk/about-us/what-we-do/

Highleyman, L. (2018). A Guide To Clinical Trials. [ebook] San Francisco AIDS Foundation. Available at: http://betablog.org/wp-content/uploads/2012/07/GuidetoclinicaltrialsPartl.pdf

Glen, S. (2017). Primary Endpoint, Surrogate & Secondary Endpoints. [online] Statistics How To. Available at: https://www.statisticshowto.datasciencecentral.com/primary-endpoint/

GOV.UK (2014). Good Clinical Practice for Clinical Trials. Available from: https://www.gov.uk/guidance/good-clinical-practice-for-clinical-trials

Health Research Authority. (2018). *Roles and responsibilities.* [online] Available at: https://www.hra.nhs.uk/planning-and-improving-research/research-planning/roles-and-responsibilities/

Health Research Authority. (2018). *Protocol.* [online] Available at: https://www.hra.nhs.uk/planning-and-improving-research/research-planning/protocol/

Kee, J. L and Hayes, Evelyn R. (2003). Pharmacology: A Nursing process Approach. Fourth Edition. USA: Elsevier Science

MHA Online (2019). Clinical Research Associate (CRA): A Day in the Life of a Clinical Research Associate. [online] mhaonline. Available at: https://www.mhaonline.com/blog/day-in-the-life-of-a-clinical-research-associate .

NIHR. (n.d.). *CRN Portfolio.* [online] Available at: https://www.nihr.ac.uk/researchers/collaborations-services-and-support-for-your-research/run-your-study/crn-portfolio.htm

University of Bath. (2019). *Research Governance.* [online] Available at: http://www.bath.ac.uk/health/brd/research-governance/

U.S. Food and Drug Administration. (1998). *Institutional Review Boards Frequently Asked Questions.* [online] Available at: https://www.fda.gov/regulatory-information/search-fda-guidance-documents/institutional-review-boards-frequently-asked-questions

Weatherspoon, D. (2018). Clinical Trial Phases: What Happens in Phase 0, I, II, III, and IV. [online] Healthline. Available at: https://www.healthline.com/health/clinical-trial-phases

World Health Organization. (2018). *Clinical trials.* [online] Available at: https://www.who.int/topics/clinical_trials/en/

# ABOUT THE AUTHOR

Ed Carbonell is an experienced registered nurse in the UK. He currently works as a nurse educator and has a freelance contract in clinical research in one of the hospitals in London. He has been involved in various clinical trials in the past working as a research nurse in the areas of inflammatory bowel disease, rheumatology, stroke, and cancer. He also once served as a quality improvement project vice chair in one of the NHS Trusts in the UK.

Printed in Poland
by Amazon Fulfillment
Poland Sp. z o.o., Wrocław